PICTURE FACTS
NIGHT SKY

N.S. Barrett

Franklin Watts

London   New York   Sydney   Toronto

Published by:

Franklin Watts
96 Leonard Street
London EC2A 4RH

Franklin Watts Australia
14 Mars Road
Lane Cove
NSW 2066

ISBN: Paperback edition 0 7496 0647 9
Hardback edition: 0 86313 286 3

Copyright © 1985 Franklin Watts

Paperback edition 1991

Hardback edition published
in the Picture Library series.

Printed in Singapore

Designed by
Barrett & Willard

Photographs by
NASA
Hale Observatories
Royal Astronomical Society
Royal Observatory, Edinburgh
US Naval Observatory, Washington
N.S. Barrett Collection
Robin Kerrod
Communications Unlimited/Crispin
Jones

Illustration by
Mike Saunders
Stuart Willard

Technical Consultant
Robin Kerrod

PICTURE FACTS

NIGHT SKY

Contents

Introduction

At night, the sky is alive with twinkling stars. On a clear night, you can see about 3,000 stars with the naked eye. With a telescope or binoculars, you can see many thousands more.

The study of the stars and the heavens is called astronomy. People who study the stars are called astronomers.

△ On a clear night, you could probably see only six or seven of these stars with the naked eye. This picture, taken from a powerful telescope, reveals thousands in just a small section of sky.

The brightest object in the night sky is the Moon. Next comes the planet Venus, which looks like a very bright star. Sometimes you can see meteors, or shooting stars.

Powerful telescopes are able to show us distant galaxies, which contain millions of stars. All the individual stars we can see belong to our own Galaxy. Astronomers divide the sky into groups of stars called constellations.

△ It is easy to see from this picture why our own Galaxy is called the Milky Way. The light from millions of stars produces this milky white effect. The streak across the picture is the path of an artificial satellite. It moved across the sky during the time the photograph was taken.

The constellations

People in the northern and southern halves, or hemispheres, of the world see different parts of the night sky. Some constellations may be seen from both hemispheres, but many can be seen only from one or the other.

The constellations have Latin names. These go back to ancient times, when stargazers saw the shapes formed by star groups as characters or creatures from stories, or as simple animals or things.

There are over 80 constellations in all. The star maps on these pages show the most important ones.

Northern Hemisphere

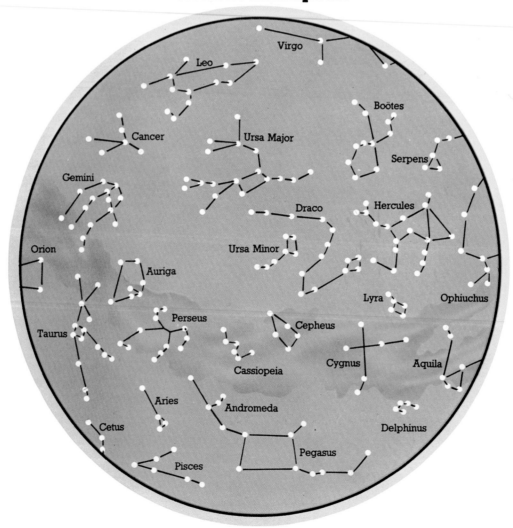

Most constellation names have meanings, although some, such as Hercules, are just names. The meanings of the names of the constellations shown on the charts are as follows:

Aquarius, Water-Bearer
Aquila, Eagle
Aries, Ram
Auriga, Charioteer
Boötes, Herdsman
Cancer, Crab
Canis Major, Great Dog
Capricornus, Sea Goat

Carina, Keel
Centaurus, Centaur
Cetus, Whale
Corvus, Crow
Crux, Southern Cross
Cygnus, Swan
Delphinus, Dolphin
Draco, Dragon
Gemini, Twins
Grus, Crane (bird)
Hydrus, Little Snake
Leo, Lion
Lepus, Hare
Libra, Scales
Lyra, Lyre
Octans, Octant (instrument)

Ophiuchus, Serpent-Bearer
Pavo, Peacock
Pegasus, Flying Horse
Pisces, Fishes
Piscis Austrinus, Southern Fish
Puppis, Poop (of ship)
Sagittarius, Archer
Scorpius, Scorpion
Serpens, Serpent
Taurus, Bull
Triangulum Australe, Southern Triangle
Ursa Major, Great Bear
Ursa Minor, Little Bear
Vela, Sails
Virgo, Virgin

Southern Hemisphere

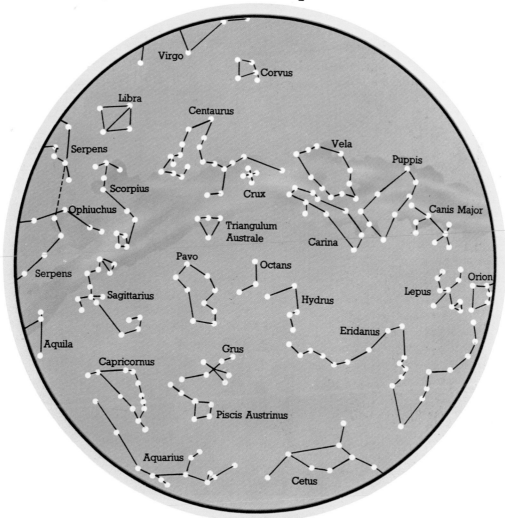

Studying the heavens

Astronomers map the night sky by imagining a vast globe around the Earth which they call the celestial sphere. It has an equator and north and south poles.

As the Earth spins around, it seems to us that the celestial sphere is turning. That is why the stars appear to move very slowly across the night sky.

▽ The drawing shows the stars of the constellation Ursa Major or the Great Bear. The seven stars joined up with blue lines form the Plough, or Big Dipper. This is one of the easiest groups to find in northern skies.

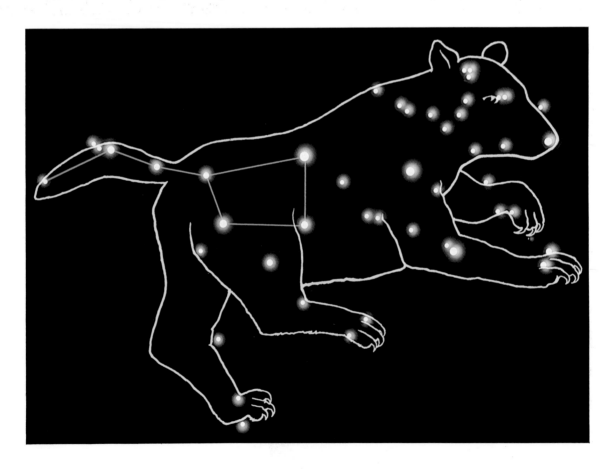

The stars are so far away that from one year to the next they are in the same position in the sky in relation to the Earth. If you look at the sky at exactly the same time on two nights, you will see the stars in almost exactly the same position.

△ Large telescopes are housed in observatories. The dome is opened up at night so that astronomers can observe the heavens.

Astronomers study the heavens with huge telescopes housed in buildings called observatories. People who study the stars as a hobby are called amateur astronomers.

Two main kinds of telescopes are used for looking at the stars. A refracting telescope uses lenses to gather the light. A reflecting telescope uses a mirror. The power of a telescope depends on the size of its main lens or mirror.

There are other ways of studying the heavens. Radio telescopes collect radio waves from distant stars and galaxies. Spacecraft telescopes study other radiations such as X-rays.

△ One of the world's great telescopes, the Hale Reflector at Mount Palomar, in California. The diameter of its mirror is over 500 cm (200 in).

◁ Telescopes used by amateur astronomers have mirrors or lenses ranging from about 7.5 cm (3 in) to 25 cm (10 in) in diameter. This one has a 21 cm ($8\frac{1}{4}$ in) mirror.

The changing Moon

The Moon shines brilliantly in the night sky. Yet it has no light of its own. All the Moon's light is reflected from the Sun.

The Moon revolves around the Earth. As it does so, it keeps the same face towards the Earth. Sometimes we see the whole of the Moon lit up. At other times we see only a part of the Moon.

▽ The full Moon as seen through a powerful telescope. The dark areas are the flat plains called maria or seas. The light areas are highlands. Many large craters are also visible.

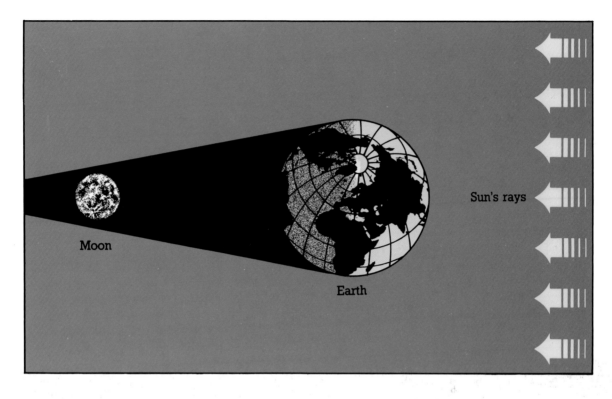

Moon

Earth

Sun's rays

The amount of the Moon we see changes from full to new (very little) and back again during the month it takes to orbit the Earth. The changing faces of the Moon are called its phases. A new Moon is sometimes just visible because the Earth reflects light on to it.

With powerful binoculars, you can see craters and mountains on the Moon. Telescopes give a fine view of the Moon's surface.

△ The Moon is eclipsed when it passes through the Earth's shadow. The Earth blocks out the Sun's rays and the surface of the Moon becomes dark.

Wandering stars

The word "planet" comes from an ancient Greek word meaning wanderer. The planets are sometimes called wandering stars. Unlike the stars, they do not have fixed positions in the heavens, but seem to wander about the sky.

The planets do not have any light of their own. Like the Moon, they shine by reflecting the Sun's rays. There are nine planets, including the Earth that move around the Sun.

▽ The planet Mars as seen through a powerful telescope. You can make out the ice caps and other markings on the planet's surface.

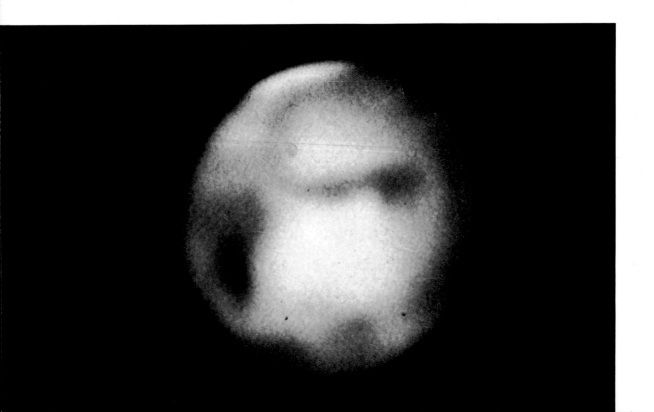

The brightest of the planets as we see them is Venus, which is the nearest one to Earth. It may often be seen just before sunrise in the east or at sunset in the west, when it shines brilliantly in the darkening sky.

The next brightest planets are Mars and Jupiter. Mars has a reddish-orange tinge. Jupiter appears white in the night sky.

△ Jupiter can be seen with the naked eye and looks like a bright star. This picture was taken from a space probe but you can see many of Jupiter's surface details with an amateur telescope.

Stars and galaxies

When you begin to explore the night sky, you start off with an easily recognizable constellation such as the Great Bear in northern skies or Crux in the south. You can then pick out other groups of stars.

The only galaxies that can be seen with the naked eye are the Magellanic clouds and the Andromeda galaxy.

△ A photograph of the Large Magellanic Cloud taken with a powerful telescope. This is one of the closest galaxies to our own and can be seen by the naked eye as a small misty patch but only in southern skies.

The constellations are groups of stars as we see them. But they only appear to be close together – in our line of sight. If they could be seen from a different part of our Galaxy, the same stars would not form a group at all.

There are, however, true groups of stars in space. Groups called star clusters are made up of hundreds or thousands of stars.

△ Star clusters are groups of stars that are close to each other in space, rather than just looking close together from Earth. The picture shows the double cluster in Perseus, also known as the Sword-Handle.

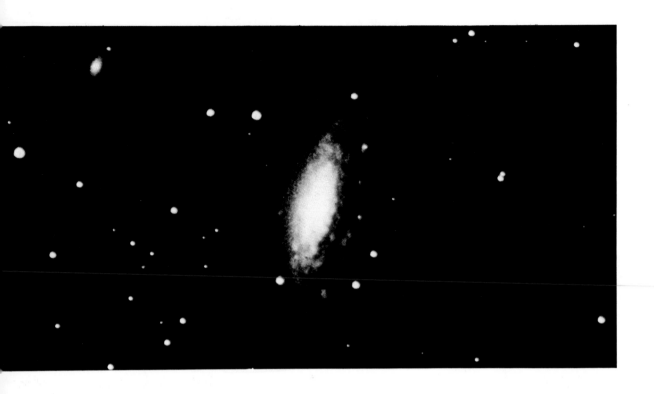

Astronomers have devised a scale of brightness for stars. The brightest stars as we see them are of 1st magnitude, the next brightest of 2nd magnitude and so on. These are called apparent magnitudes because they measure how bright a star appears to us.

You can see stars down to the 6th magnitude with the naked eye. Some telescopes can detect stars fainter then the 25th magnitude.

△ A distant galaxy shows up as a bright patch of light when viewed through a large telescope.

Shapes in the sky

There is more to see in the night sky than planets and stars. There are misty patches of light in various shapes and colours. These are called nebulae, which means clouds.

Astronomers used to call any misty patch a nebula. Some of these were later found to be star clusters or galaxies. But many nebulae really are clouds – of gas or dust.

▽ The Horsehead Nebula in Orion. This is a dark nebula, a dense cloud of gas and dust that gives out no light itself but can be seen against the bright nebula behind it.

△ The Rosette Nebula is a great glowing cloud of dust to be seen in the Milky Way.

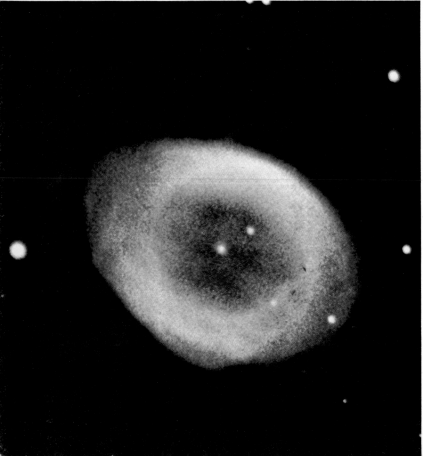

◁ The Ring Nebula in Lyra was formed when a dying star shed its outer layer of gas.

Only a few nebulae can be seen with the naked eye. These include the Great Nebula in the constellation of Orion and the Lagoon Nebula in Sagittarius.

Particles that exist in space between the stars are called interstellar matter. This makes up the gas and dust of the nebulae.

△ The Veil Nebula was formed by the remains of an explosion of a giant star.

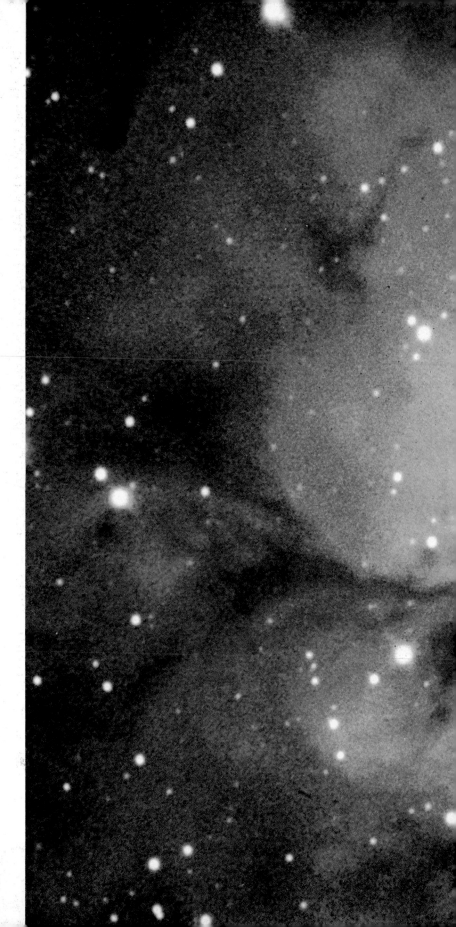

▷ The Trifid Nebula, one of the most exciting sights in the night sky. A long-exposure photograph taken through a large telescope reveals a variety of shapes and colours. The nebula consists of vast clouds of hydrogen gas streaked with dark channels of dust. Bright stars inside the nebula cause it to glow.

The Trifid may be located in the constellation of Sagittarius and may just be seen with the aid of a pair of good binoculars.

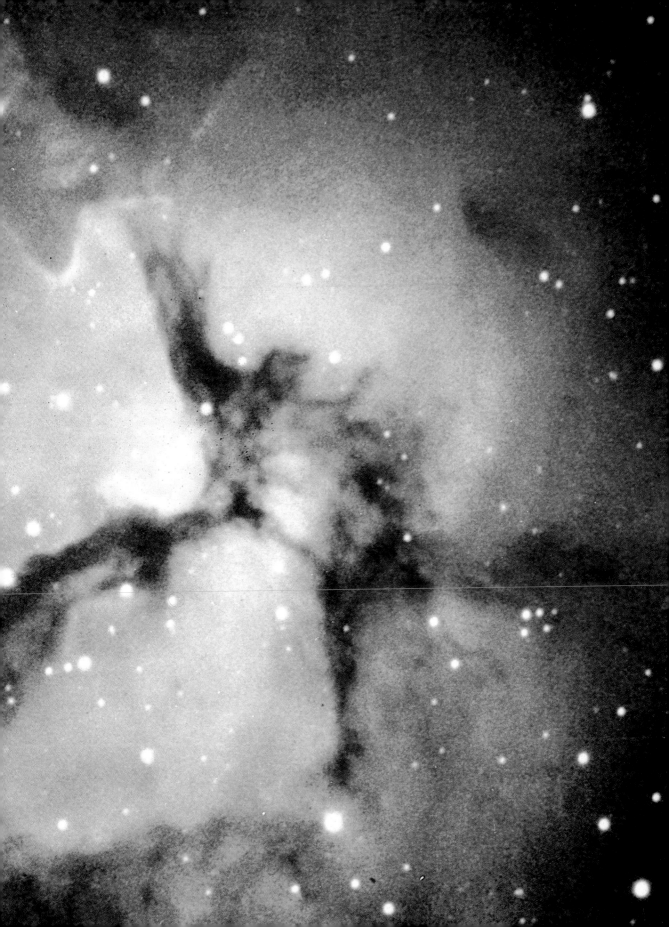

Comets

Comets belong to the Solar System. They are made up of ice and dust. Their orbits take them a long way from the Sun.

When a comet comes close to the Sun it begins to glow with reflected light. Gases and dust are given off forming a glowing head, or coma, and a tail. The tails of some comets stretch out for millions of kilometres.

△ Comet Ikeya-Seki made a spectacular appearance in 1965, when this photograph was taken. Its tail is seen to spread diagonally across the night sky.

Shooting stars

A meteor is the bright streak caused when a piece of rock enters the Earth's atmosphere from space and burns up. It glows brightly as it is heated by the friction of the air. This is why meteors are often known as shooting stars.

Most meteors burn up in the atmosphere. Large ones may even reach the Earth's surface, and the particles are called meteorites.

▽ A meteor hurtles through the Earth's atmosphere, glowing white from the heat of friction. Most meteors burn out before they reach the ground and this one can be seen breaking up.

The story of astronomy

Ancient stargazers

People have always gazed up at the night sky, pondering the secrets of the universe. Over 3,000 years ago the Chinese charted the positions of the stars and recorded eclipses.

The ancient Greeks tried to explain the movements of the heavenly bodies. Pythagoras worked out that the Earth is round. Aristarchus suggested that the Earth and the other planets might travel around the Sun. But most ancient stargazers thought that the Earth was the centre of the universe and that the planets and the Sun revolved around it.

△ People are pointing to Halley's Comet in this famous scene from English history before the Norman invasion of 1066.

Earth at the centre

In about AD 100, a Greek astronomer called Ptolemy wrote the *Almagest*. This famous book, which included the work of earlier astronomers as well as Ptolemy's own ideas, placed the Earth at the centre of the universal system. It was another 1,400 years before astronomers began to doubt it.

Birth of modern astronomy

The first man to question the old and accepted ideas was a Polish astronomer, Nicolaus Copernicus. The work of a Danish astronomer, Tycho Brahe and later of his German assistant Johannes Kepler, supported the views of Copernicus. These advances

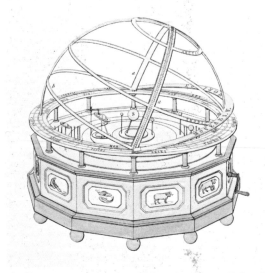

△ An orrery is a mechanical model of the Solar System. Orreries were used to demonstrate the motions of the planets by the turn of a handle.

marked the beginning of astronomy as we know it today.

New discoveries
The Italian astronomer Galileo was the first to use a telescope for studying the heavens. He made many important discoveries.

In the late 1600s, the English scientist Isaac Newton discovered the law of gravitation – that every object in the universe attracts every other object. The strength of the attraction depends on the masses, or weights, of the objects and their distance apart. This law explains the motions of planets and comets.

Another important discovery of Newton's was that visible light can be broken down into a rainbow of colours. Later scientists used this idea to study light from the stars and learn much more about them.

Astronomy today
With modern telescopes and techniques, astronomers make many exciting new discoveries. Computers help them to make complicated calculations. Radio telescopes, with their huge dish aerials, collect information from parts of the universe out of reach of optical telescopes.

More great advances have been made since the beginning of space flight. Telescopes in space are not hindered by the Earth's atmosphere and can "see" much farther than land-based ones. We know so much more about our universe than the ancient stargazers did, but we often still look at the sky in wonder because there is so much more to learn.

△ **A radio telescope.**

Facts and records

△ Indians overawed as the Moon disappears during an eclipse.

Why stars "twinkle"

Looked at from the Earth, stars appear to twinkle. Starlight is bent as it travels through the moving layers of air in the Earth's atmosphere. This causes it to vary in brightness, which is the reason for the twinkling.

Columbus's eclipse trick

In the past, the ability to predict an eclipse has proved valuable to explorers. A famous case occurred on Christopher Columbus's last expedition to the Americas. He was marooned on the island of Jamaica and badly needed food for his men. But relations with the native Indians were not friendly. So he used the "eclipse trick". He found from his almanac that there was to be a total eclipse of the Moon. He told the Indians that God would punish them by taking away the light unless they provided food. When the light began to disappear, they were terrified and hurried to the ships with provisions.

Glossary

Astronomy
The scientific study of the stars, planets and other heavenly bodies.

Celestial sphere
An imaginary sphere, or hollow ball, surrounding the Earth, on which we see the stars.

Comet
A body that moves around the Sun in a very elongated path. Some comets take thousands of years to make a complete orbit. Halley's Comet is the only bright comet that orbits the Sun in less than 100 years.

Constellation
A named group of stars, one of 88 officially recognized.

Galaxy
A huge system consisting of billions of stars and other matter such as gas and dust.

Magnitude
A measure of star brightness.

Meteor
The streak caused when any body, from a tiny particle to a large rock, enters the Earth's atmosphere and glows with heat. Meteors are also called shooting stars.

Nebula
A cloud of gas and particles in space. Some nebulae (the plural) are bright, shining with their own light or the reflected light of nearby stars. Others are dark and are seen only because they blot out the light of stars beyond them.

Observatory
A scientific institution for studies in astronomy. Observatories are equipped with telescopes and other instruments used for studying the heavens.

Orbit
The path one body takes around a larger body. The planets orbit the Sun.

Planets
The nine large bodies that orbit the Sun.

Radio telescope
An instrument used for studying radio waves from space.

Star cluster
A group of stars that move together through space.

Index